SPARTAN
PROJECT MANAGEMENT

A NEW PROJECT MANAGER'S GUIDE
Second Edition - 2016

SPARTAN
PROJECT MANAGEMENT

A NEW PROJECT MANAGER'S GUIDE

Second Edition - 2016

SADIQ SOMJEE

Published by GeoEdge Consulting Ltd.

Vancouver, Canada.

SPARTAN PROJECT MANAGEMENT

A New Project Manager's Guide

Copyright © 2012-2016 by Sadiq Somjee

First Edition 2012

Second Edition 2016

somjeeNotes.blogspot.ca

Print Book ISBN-13: 978-1469981833
Print Book ISBN-10: 1469981831

CONTENTS

ACKNOWLEDGMENTS

I am grateful to all those who supported me and worked with me on projects, you were all critical success factors. Without your dedication, the projects would have surely failed.

"Begin at the beginning,' the King
said, very gravely, 'and go on till
you come to the end: then stop."

Lewis Carroll

Alice in Wonderland

PREFACE TO THE 2ND EDITION

This book is not a certification guide; it comes from real world experience. It uses examples of actual IT projects and simplifies project management to the basic elements, stripping the jargon to make it a practical guide for budding project managers. It is what you need to get the job done.

In this second edition I am sharing 30 years of my experience managing IT projects. The first edition was designed to be a project management cookbook. Although the book still has the same project recipes, they have been enhanced and revised. New topics on project creativity and project ecosystems have been added.

Much has changed since the first edition. On the professional side I completed more projects, helped initiate, strategize and orchestrate a number of technology projects related to CRM, data warehousing, business intelligence, cloud hosting and mobile devices. These projects had stakeholders from interdisciplinary teams and came from a range of geographic and cultural backgrounds.

In 2015, I fulfilled my dream to publish a graphic novel called *The Cheese In Between*. It is a story about a farm boy who gets thrown into a project management role in a large corporation. The creative process of developing a visual story surfaced deep insights about people and communication in project management, which I reveal in this edition.

In every iterative and creative process, the next generation product only gets better and streamlined. I also worked to add more diagrams, cartoons and examples to make this book easy to digest and make it a practical read.

Sincerely

Sadiq Somjee

INTRODUCTION

This guide is for accidental project managers who find themselves in charge. It will provide you with the core set of skills required to manage projects in any environment.

Across industries, variations of the Spartan philosophy emerged due to project cost overruns and as a need to be competitive in challenging economic times. Most project veterans know that project failure is a result of poorly defined requirements, overbuilding, scope creep, and failure to manage and control the project.

The Spartan project approach developed over several years while working for both midsized companies and large corporations. This guide provides a project management framework for new project managers in a practical and simple manner using examples and templates. It is my hope that you can take these templates and immediately apply them to your projects.

A holistic approach to project management will be shown in five steps. This practical and concise guide will get you jump-started as a project manager. It can be read on its own, or it can be used a companion to more formal textbooks. When you have finished, you will have a better understanding of how to start, manage, and deliver a successful project using a simple communication dashboard. Specifically, this guide will cover:

- Collecting the right information
- Developing a project plan
- Managing and executing a project
- Transitioning and closing a project
- A project checklist

Books, certifications and online material can be overwhelming and impractical, especially if you are new to project management. This book will kick start you in the right direction with simple project management tools and techniques.

The techniques in this guide have been applied to both small projects and multi-million dollar projects over my thirty years in the project management business. All projects require coordination of people, equipment, suppliers, costs and schedules. Most of the projects are time critical and cost sensitive for a number of reasons such as company acquisitions, project rescues, or business improvements.

The core, project management techniques shown, will ease your anxiety about managing projects and provide you with the tools to complete a project successfully. A successful conclusion means that the project achieved its goals, was completed on time, and delivered on or under budget.

Start with the end

> *"What we call the beginning is often the end. And to make an end is to make a beginning. The end is where we start from."*
>
> *T.S. Eliot*

A project has a finite life; it has a beginning and an end. Once the project is completed, it must be closed. A seasoned project manager starts with the end in mind. You need to clearly describe and share what the end looks like, so everyone has the same end vision in mind.

According to the Project Management Institute (PMI), a project has five key processes: initiating, planning, executing, monitoring and controlling, and closing, which in this guide are referred to as steps. The secret to a successful project is in how the steps are executed in practice.

During the initiation step, you will discover and document the project goals, objectives, and desired outcomes. Use this discovery time to understand the players and the project scope. The project sponsor is the most important person to interact with during initiation, as the sponsor will describe the end vision. The sponsor is the person, who has requested the project and is the one paying for the work.

In the planning stage, the project plan will be developed, costs will be estimated, and resource requirements will be identified. You will be gathering information from subject matter experts to define the tasks and estimate the effort.

Project risks will need to be identified and strategies to mitigate them will be developed. There will be expectations from management and the team, which you will need to understand and manage.

On approval of the project plan from the sponsor, the execution step begins. During this stage, you will be acquiring your teams and preparing the foundation to start the work. It is here that the work is actually carried out, work such as signing contracts, purchasing material, installing hardware, and building houses.

In the managing step, production is monitored, quality is controlled, project team members are held to task, and risks are actively managed. The scope and schedules are managed and controlled. At this stage, there will be a high degree of interaction with various teams. You will be communicating across teams to verify all of the project parts integrate into the whole.

An example will be used to describe the 5 steps, from initiation to close, to demonstrate how to apply the project management tools and techniques presented. It is based on a blend of actual projects for which I had responsibility. It is a typical project involving people, distributed offices, vendors and technology.

On completion, this guide will leave you with a practical understanding of project management and tools you can apply. The foundation in this guide will also provide you with the knowledge to explore other project management areas further, areas such as cost management, quality control, communication and risk management.

SPARTAN PROJECT MANAGEMENT

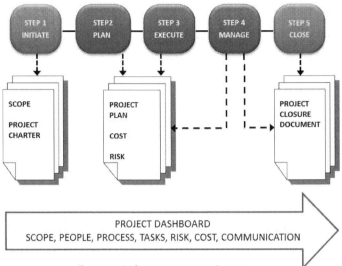

Figure 1 – Project Management Process

Throughout the lifecycle of the project, you will be exposed to people, products and business practices. The project might be related to technology, health care, natural resources, entertainment, finance or other industries. Use this time to understand both the business and the people.

If you are an employee, you have the advantage of already knowing the people, the business and the company culture. As an employee, use your company knowledge and network when initiating, executing, managing and closing the project.

Each company has a different culture and you will need to adapt your style to theirs. For example, some companies may be less formal and may not require detailed reports, while others may have well-established project management practices, requiring formal and regular reporting. Regardless of the company culture or style, the five steps presented must be followed, and there should be effective and constant communication in order to deliver a successful project.

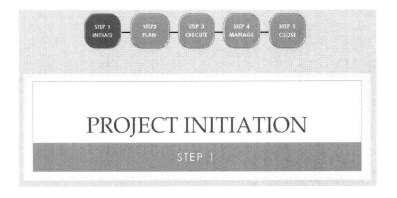

STEP 1 - INITIATE

First comes thought; then organization of that thought, into ideas and plans; then transformation of those plans into reality. The beginning, as you will observe, is in your imagination."

Napoleon Hill

Project initiation is a quest for discovery, where you seek to understand the mission, the players and the scope. Project initiation is the point at which you are gathering information about the size, people, processes, current situation and interfaces related to your project deliverables.

Interview the project sponsors and document your findings in the project charter.

In our example, the new mobile devices are deployed to field offices to collect inventory information on industrial equipment for sale. The field staff will collect information on equipment type, manufacturer, last service date, model, and other information. They are happy with the current mobile devices and are not keen to change. However, the old mobile devices are breaking down and are too expensive to support. This is the key reason the director of field operations has requested the replacement.

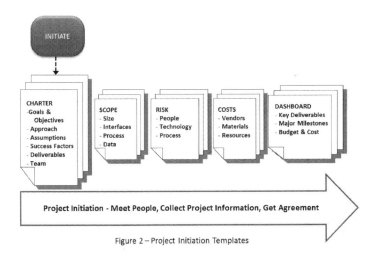

Figure 2 – Project Initiation Templates

This is all the project information you have been given by the director. The director wants you to look at the current situation and provide him with a plan and cost to replace the aging mobile devices. At this stage the project information is still ambiguous and needs more detail. You need to investigate the requirements further. Do not oversell and manage expectations from the start. As PM managing expectations means managing scope, cost and time.

If you do oversell, you will be held accountable to deliver on that commitment. Managers will push you to raise the bar, do it with care. Discuss the cost, time, resources and technology to deliver that vision. This is an opportunity for you and the company, so be optimistic. Also stand your ground diplomatically and give careful consideration to the scope, complexity and timeline proposed.

You must understand the scope of the project, before submitting plan and cost information. Scope deals with size and complexity. For example, how many locations are involved? Will software for the mobile devices need to be developed or purchased? Is the data used in other systems? Are there other areas the project may affect? What data is being collected today and what additional data is required in the future? What are the expectations upon completion?

The purpose of the project charter is to answer these questions, and to formalize the findings in a document so you can establish a common understanding.

Project Charter

The project charter document consists of project scope, goals and objectives, assumptions, risks, success factors, project deliverables, resources, budget, communication plan and a high level schedule with key milestones. The charter has enough detail to get a good sense of what it will take to deliver the project. More details will be fleshed out during the planning phase. Review the charter with experts and sponsors to get a realistic picture of the project.

Questions to Ask

Remember that the sponsor(s) are the ones who initiated, and are paying for the project. Therefore, you must clarify their request and expectations in the project charter. Get information about the current situation from the existing documentation and the people in the company. Prepare a list of investigative questions to ask the project sponsors, for example:

1. What is your vision for this project?
2. What are the problems today and how will the project solve these problems?
3. What are the critical success factors?
4. What are the deliverables of the project?
5. Who are the stakeholders (people impacted by the project)?
6. Who should we involve as part of the project team?
7. What is the impact to the end users?
8. Do you foresee any issues with this project?
9. Has this project been attempted before?
10. What do the project outcomes look like on completion?
11. What is the budget?

12. What are your expectations?

Design the questions in a way that will help you complete the project charter. In the project charter, you will also be defining the project team with direction from the project sponsors. This team will then be acquired and secured later during the execution phase. Based on the project scope and deliverables, determine if you have representation from each of the project areas. For example, for each field office you will need a representative to assist you with product selection, requirements and training. In addition, you will need members from finance and inventory to help develop the reports. The project will also require technical people to help install the wireless networks and develop the data integration applications into the financial and inventory systems. As you define the team with the sponsors, consider the work and ask for resources with the required skills.

At the initial stage keep the questions broad and open to allow the sponsor and stakeholders to articulate their vision. At this stage your role is to ask investigative questions without presenting solutions.

As part of the project charter, prepare a scope diagram and describe the project components. In this case, it is the field offices, the number of mobile device units, and the data upload process to the inventory and financial systems.

Example Project Charter

Project Charter	Description
Scope	Replace the aging mobile devices in 6 field offices with new mobile devices. Improve the process of uploading the mobile device data to head office. Load and integrate the mobile device data into the enterprise financial and inventory systems. Develop reports.
Business Goals and Objectives	• To improve the uptime, safety, service and life of the field equipment (trucks, cranes, tractors). • To reduce the cost and time lost to problems with mobile data collection devices in the field. • Collect more relevant data to the business and improve the data quality. • Eliminate the support risk and cost of old technology.
Project Approach	• Conduct a situation assessment (discovery). • Develop a project plan. • Develop a delivery plan. • Execute the approved plan. • Close the project
Assumptions	• Availability of field personnel to test and evaluate the devices. • Availability of resources to write the interfaces to load the mobile device data into the financial and inventory systems
Critical Success Factors	• Seamless replacement of devices with no disruption to current business operations. • Ease of use of the mobile devices and adoption by field personnel. • Meet or exceed existing functionality.

Project Deliverables	• Replace mobile devices with new models. • Improve equipment data collection and processes. • Train field personnel. • Implement site wireless infrastructure. • Transmit mobile device data to head office. • Upload data to the inventory and finance systems. • Improve financial and field inventory reporting.
Project Team and Responsibilities	• Project Manager reporting to the Director of Field Operations and the Director of Finance (sponsors). The project manager will report monthly and escalate major issues or scope changes to the project sponsors. • The working group headed by the project manager and will include finance, inventory, technical and site supervisors. The working group will connect weekly to ensure project success. • Site field supervisors will be involved to help select, test the mobile device technology, and secure assistance from field personnel as required. • Inventory and finance application programmers will assist with the report specifications. • Subject matter experts in field coordination and equipment maintenance will be engaged as required by the project team. • The project manager and project team will be accountable to the project sponsors.
Project Budget	$750,000
Initial Risk Analysis and Assessment	• Adoption and acceptance of the new mobile devices and data collection software by field personnel. • Detail cost breakdowns are not available and the budget has not been verified.

Project Schedule	• Phase 1 (Q1)
	    ○ Complete project charter and preliminary scope.
	    ○ Conduct a project discovery.
	    ○ Complete detailed scope.
	    ○ Complete project plan.
	    ○ Complete cost estimates.
	    ○ Complete an initial risk plan.
	    ○ Present approach and options.

As you investigate further, you discover that the mobile device replacement is expected to improve data quality, data collection and data integration into the financial and inventory systems. Document these expectations in the project charter under goals and objectives.

At this point in the project, you do not have enough information to build a project plan without further investigation. What you have completed is an initial assessment. You have presented an approach to gather more information to develop a project plan, investigate costs, assess risks and develop an overall project approach. You have reviewed and discussed the project charter and scope with the project team and the project sponsors. In Step 1, you have only committed to the delivery of the project plan, cost estimates, initial risk assessment and a project approach, because the project sponsor has not approved the plan and cost.

Discovery

A discovery is conducted to find out more about the project; gather requirements on how the data is currently collected and get more details for each location. This investigation will give you more information on the effort. For example, the large field offices will require more time to test, train, and deploy the mobile devices, while smaller sites will require less time.

In our example, large sites have a lot of equipment on location and currently have 50 or more mobile devices. The medium site has 20 mobile devices and the small ones have less than 10. Each one of these sites will require a different amount of effort to train and rollout the mobile devices.

The existing mobile devices are used to collect information on make, model, year, warranty, last service date, mileage and various other equipment attributes. The data collected on the mobile devices needs to be transmitted to the head office. The data is required by both the financial system and the inventory system. Both of these systems produce reports required by management.

The number of field offices, data, and flow of information along with the end use of the data, provides the critical information required for developing the scope.

By conducting the initial investigation, you will have identified the existing systems, people and skills. You will also have important information about what the delivered project will look like and have some idea about time, budget and resource constraints. Include what you know about the project and the assumptions in the project charter, so you can confirm your understanding with the project sponsors.

Discuss the project charter with the project team, make modifications, and do the same with the project sponsors. Until you get agreement from the project sponsors, keep reviewing and refining the project charter. It is critical to get signoff from the sponsors by signature in the project charter, stating approval of the project as described. The project charter is a document you will refer to throughout the life of the project. It will also be used when closing the project to verify the deliverables were completed and that goals and objectives were met. The project charter is an important document, which must be absolutely clear and accepted by the sponsors, before proceeding to the next step. Failing to do this will inevitably lead to misunderstanding and possibly a failed project.

Scope

As project manager, you need to be in control of project scope throughout the life of the project. A change in scope will have an impact on time and cost. Scope covers locations, size, people, equipment, information flow, processes, report specifications, software requirements, data requirements and project deliverables. Describe and diagram the components and information flow in your scope document (figure 3).

The project objective is to replace the mobile devices in six field offices. The new mobile devices will have custom software to collect equipment information and then transmit this information to the head office.

Develop a narrative to go with the scope diagram, for example:

New mobile devices will be evaluated, customized and deployed to each of the six sites. Wireless access points will also be set up at the six sites to transmit the data. The equipment data collected will be integrated and updated in both the financial and inventory system at head office. Equipment reports will be customized, based on requirements from the field supervisors, financial staff and inventory staff. The new mobile devices will be designed and programmed to collect equipment inventory information. Customized training will be delivered to each of the six sites. The data will be sent to headquarters over a secure wireless access point on each site.

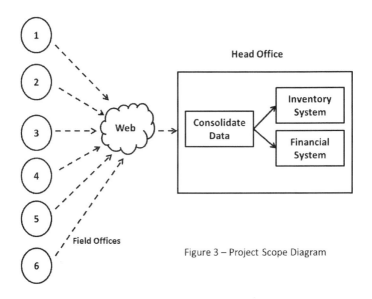

Figure 3 – Project Scope Diagram

In larger organizations, business analysts and system analysts can assist with describing the scope. In smaller organizations, you may not have that benefit and as a result will need to collect the scope information from subject matter experts yourself. Regardless, the project manager must have a good understanding of the people, processes and technology in the scope. To plan, execute and manage the project, this knowledge is necessary. As you develop the scope, consider and collect information on:

1. The number of locations
2. The number of users by location
3. Inputs and data to be collected
4. Mobile device to head office data flows
5. Integration and relationships with other systems
6. Outputs and reports

Do Not Commit

At the initiation stage, there is not enough information to make commitments on budget, project deliverables or time frame. Schedule, cost, scope, quality, risk and customer satisfaction are related. A change in one has an impact on the other. For example, if the time is shortened, it will impact the scope, and perhaps the risk and quality. This will compromise customer satisfaction. In the end, all people will remember is how poorly the project was delivered. To avoid this situation, validate the project plan, scope and costs before committing. Remember your reputation is key to your long term earning.

Get Sign Off

Make sure that everyone takes ownership of the project charter by including feedback in the document. This way, you will have commitment and support from the team during the life of the project. After all, the project charter is documented, based on instructions and input from the sponsors and the project team. Communication and openness are critical with the sponsors, the project team and the stakeholders. Share, develop and adjust the project charter with the project team and sponsors. Get agreement on the scope, deliverables, goals and objectives. In case there is disagreement, the project sponsors always have the final word. The project charter facilitates a common end vision. The charter is your GPS and destination roadmap.

Dashboard

At the initiation phase, start with the end in mind, do this by putting together a project closure dashboard. This document will describe the end vision for all to share. The key is to develop this document in collaboration with the project sponsor and project stakeholders. You will find most of the closure information in the project charter. This onc page dashboard will be used to convey the project status to the project sponsors throughout the life of the project.

Create the dashboard by extracting information from the project charter document. Insert an acceptance column to the right. At this stage the "Accepted" column is still to be determined (TBD) and will be updated as the project progresses.

The project charter and dashboard simply clarify the scope and "what" needs to be done. The details of "how" this will be achieved are developed in the next planning step. The project could be a real estate community development, a start-up of a distribution warehouse or a technology upgrade. The charter and dashboard capture the sponsor's expectations.

Project Dashboard	Description	Accepted
Project Definitions and Scope	Replace the aging mobile devices in 6 field offices with new mobile devices. Improve the process of uploading the mobile device data to head office. Load the mobile device data into the enterprise financial and inventory systems. Develop Reports.	TBD
Business Goals and Objectives	• Improve the equipment uptime, safety, service and life of the field equipment (trucks, cranes, tractors). • Reduce the cost and time lost to problems with mobile data collection devices in the field. • Collect more relevant data to the business and improve the data quality. • Eliminate the support risk and cost of old technology.	TBD
Critical Success Factors	• Seamless replacement of devices with no disruption to current business operations. • Ease of use of the mobile devices and adoption by field personnel. • Meet or exceed existing functionality.	TBD
Project Deliverables	• Replace the mobile devices with new models. • Improve equipment data collection and processes. • Train field personnel. • Implement site wireless infrastructure. • Transmit mobile device data to head office. • Upload data to the inventory and finance systems. • Improve financial and field inventory reporting.	TBD
Project Schedule	• As per project plan.	TBD

In addition to the project charter information add the following task and budget dashboards:

Field Office	Mobile devices Deployed	Training Complete	Wireless Installed	Site Operational	Comment
Field Site 1	No	No	No	No	
Field Site 2	No	No	No	No	
Field Site 3	No	No	No	No	
Field Site 4	No	No	No	No	
Field Site 5	No	No	No	No	
Field Site 6	No	No	No	No	

SPARTAN PROJECT MANAGEMENT

Key Project Tasks	Complete	Comment
Devices Selected	No	Establish selection team
Software Selected	No	Determine requirements and research vendors
Software Customized	No	
Data Fields Added	No	
Field Data Collected	No	

Key Project Tasks	Complete	Comment
Inventory Report X	No	Gather requirements from the Finance department.
Inventory Report Y	No	
Financial Report A	No	
Financial Report B	No	

Budget vs. Completion	Planned	Actual Budget Used	Percent Budget Used	Percent Project Complete
	750,000	0	0%	0%

The dashboard tasks will all have a status of "No." Over time, they will change to "Yes" or the percentage of completion. These indicators will let you and the project sponsors discuss and zero in on the completed and outstanding tasks. Basically, the dashboard is a gauge to monitor and communicate progress about the project. Based on these templates, build your own dashboards for your project.

Project closure dashboard and dashboard are used interchangeably, and refer to the same template, throughout this guide. The dashboard will be used to monitor progress with the project team and sponsors throughout the life of the project. This is a key template to communicate the project status and remind the team of the agreements. If the team decides to make a change to the project and the sponsors agree, the change will need to be added as an amendment to the project charter and dashboard. In the amendment, add the date of change and the reason for the change, so time, cost and resource impacts are documented.

Summary

During the initiation phase, information is gathered on the project goals and objectives, the scope and the budget. The project manager is investigating and discovering more about the project, the business requirements and the company culture.

1. Develop the project charter and document the goals and objectives, the project team, the scope and the project deliverables.
2. Include the scope in the project charter. The scope will cover all parts of the project, such as geographic locations, departments, people, processes, data flows and technology.
3. Engage the project team and sponsors to develop the project charter and dashboard.

4. Based on the project charter, develop a project closure dashboard, which will used throughout the project as a project status communication tool.

5. Get approval and signoff on the project charter and project closure dashboard from the sponsors.

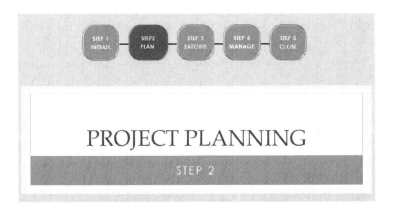

STEP2 - PLAN

If you go to work on your goals, your goals will go to work on you. If you go to work on your plan, your plan will go to work on you. Whatever good things we build end up building us."
Jim Rohn

In the planning phase, you will produce a project plan, a risk management plan and a cost breakdown. As you develop the project plan, you will be identifying risks and costs. Collect this information in a cost spreadsheet and a risk document. Some project risks may have already been identified in the scope document. For example, a risk may be that field users are reluctant to change technology.

The purpose of the project plan is to meet the project goals and objectives by completing the defined work. The plan is a working document that is designed to measure, monitor and manage tasks to achieve an end result. Work, schedules and risks are controlled, measured and monitored via the plan. The plan describes how the end will be achieved.

Divide and Conquer

To develop the project plan, you will need to break down the tasks into a Work Breakdown Structure (WBS). The scope provides a good starting point. Examples of tasks include evaluating mobile devices, developing software, selecting suppliers, testing products, developing reports, and installing wireless access points.

Ask the subject matter experts for help in breaking down the tasks. For example, the application programmers can define the tasks to develop the reports. Review the estimates with the team to make sure all tasks, such as requirements gathering, developing and testing, have been considered. Include financial accountants for report specifications, trainers to get training estimates, network experts to get estimates on installing wireless access points. The finer the breakdown of tasks, the more accurate your plan will be.

Basically, the WBS is a way to divide and conquer the project by breaking down the work into manageable tasks. These small work units will be easier to estimate and be assigned to individuals on the team. In figure 4, the project has been broken down into 4 common phases (Discovery, Design and Develop, Pilot and Test, and Implement). Your project may have different phases, but the principle is the same.

Next, break the phases down into sub tasks, starting with the major components, and then breaking them down into smaller work units. For example, the "Develop and Design" phase has 3 subtasks (2.1 Mobile Devices, 2.2 Upload, and 2.3 Reports). Then each subtask is broken down into lower level tasks. Break down the tasks into manageable work units without getting absurdly small.

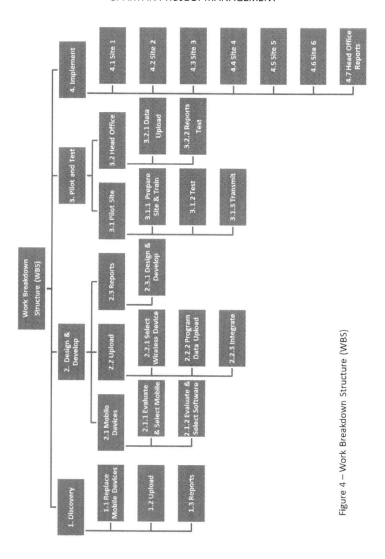

Figure 4 – Work Breakdown Structure (WBS)

Develop time estimates for the subtasks and assign them to resources (people) who have the expertise, authority or ability to deliver and complete those tasks.

Task estimates will feed into the project plan. Some tasks are dependent on others, such as the selection of the mobile device (2.1.1) and the software (2.1.2). These dependencies are important for sequencing the tasks in the project plan.

In our example, the high level tasks are to replace the mobile devices, transmit the data to the head office, upload the data and develop reports. Start with the high level tasks and break them down into phases (discovery, design and develop, pilot and test, implement.)

1. Discovery Phase

(1.1) Replace mobile devices

- Collect information on how the devices are currently used.
- Evaluate existing mobile device for likes and dislikes
- Determine how and what data is being collected

(1.2) Upload

- Current data collected

- Current issues with the upload
- Methods of data transmission to head office
- Integration into inventory and financial systems

(1.3) Reports

- List of current reports and gaps
- List of desired reports
- Determine data needs for the reports

At the end of the discovery phase, you will be able to determine the detail requirements, understand the current issues and risks. Some may be addressed with no additional time, cost or resources, while others may have an impact on the project.

2. Design and Develop Phase

(2.1) Mobile Devices

- Research, evaluate and select new mobile devices
- Research, evaluate and select mobile device software
- Determine costs
- What are the selection criteria for the mobile devices?
- Buy or develop mobile device software

(2.2) Upload

- Design a new upload process into the financial and inventory systems
- Application to capture the incoming data into a database
- Develop site wireless network requirements and cost

(2.3) Develop Reports

- Design new inventory and finance reports
- Develop reports

3. Pilot and Test Phase

(3.1) Pilot Site

- Prepare site and train (3.1.1)

  Consider all the sub tasks required for the test, such as setting up the wireless, staff training and acquiring the devices.

- Test (3.1.2)

  Include tasks such as configuring the mobile device software and sample tests.

- Transmit (3.1.3)

Conduct and verify equipment data transmission.

Test and correct data collection and reports.

(3.2) Head Office

Receive and consume data.

- Data Upload (3.2.1)

  Validate data is correctly acquired into the inventory and finance system

- Reports Test (3.2.2)

  Validate reports are correct.

Many projects require a pilot phase to validate the assumptions in the project plan and mitigate the risks before going forward. In this case, a pilot phase has been introduced, because there are cost, technology, and device functionality unknowns. Therefore, the devices, processes, new software and technology need to be field tested in an actual operations environment. At the end of this phase, you will understand the issues that may arise when you rollout the mobile devices to production. Rework and redesign may be required, as there may be issues with the devices, the software, or the acceptance of the new technology by the field staff. This risks and issues will need to be addressed and a second iteration of the pilot may be required, or the issues might be resolved before going live. Information from the pilot may require changes to the project plan at a later point.

Pilots can also be applied when changing business processes. For example if there is an existing business process a change will take time, training and acceptance. It is a good way to discover flaws, engage people and get adoption.

Before entering the implementation phase, there will be some work to get the devices, software and reports ready. Add these preliminary tasks prior to starting implementation.

4. **Implementation Phase: For each site (4.1 to 4.6), develop a plan:**

    - Site communication plan

      Advise, coordinate and communicate the training and site plan

    - Mobile device replacement plan

      - Train field staff

      - Site test

      - Switch over to the new system

    - Data transmission plan

      Ensure the wireless infrastructure is setup before site training begins

    - Upload plan

      Test the upload before the training

    - Report test plan

      - Validate data

      - Develop a report "go live" plan

The idea here is to clearly describe each task in terms of the work, the quality expectations and the outcomes.

Start with a high level project plan and break down the details with dates, time frames and assigned resources. In the planning phase, you want to create a project plan from the Work Breakdown Structure (figure 4). Notice how the project plan mirrors the WBS. Each phase is broken into work units, and each work unit is broken down into well-defined tasks. For each unique work unit:

1. Determine the effort in terms of resources and time to complete.

2. Determine which task needs to be done first based on the task dependencies.

3. Assign resources to the tasks.

4. Lay out the sequence of the project tasks and resources into a project plan (figure 5), based on resources, task dependencies and priorities.

5. Estimate the cost for each work unit. Add these costs to get the total cost estimate.

Many people think of a project plan as just a Gantt chart. A project plan is more than that; it is a set of management plans describing how each task group will be completed.

Do not worry about project management software if you are not familiar with one. Instead, you may use a spreadsheet to layout the project plan by tasks and dates. However, a project management tool does provide sophisticated features such as status reporting, cost monitoring, progress tracking, linking dependent tasks and scheduling common resources. At this point, a spreadsheet of tasks, along with the dashboard, the risk register and cost register are enough to monitor and control a project. The risk and cost registers are described in the next section. As long as the project plan keeps track of the tasks, the task progress, person responsible for the task, the start date and duration the tool used does not matter. I have seen many people using a tool and loosing sight of the project.

Do not get hung up on the tool and the process, instead focus on the deliverables and communication with the team.

	Task Name	Duration	Start	Finish	Pred	Resc
1	⊟ 1. Discovery	10 days	02 May	13 May		Joe
2	1.1 Replace Mobile Devices	3 days	02 May	04 May		Joe
3	1.2 Upload Process	2 days	05 May	06 May	2	Sam
4	1.3 Report Requirements	5 days	09 May	13 May	3	Joe
5	⊟ 2. Design & Develop	45 days	16 May	15 Jul		
6	⊟ 2.1 Mobile Devices	15 days	16 May	03 Jun		
7	2.1.1 Evaluate & Select Hardware	5 days	16 May	20 May	1	Joe
8	2.1.2 Evaluate & Select Software	10 days	23 May	03 Jun	7	Sam
9	⊟ 2.2 Upload	25 days	23 May	24 Jun		
10	2.2.1 Select Wireless Device	3 days	23 May	25 May	7	Joe
11	2.2.2 Program Data Upload	10 days	06 Jun	17 Jun	8	Sam
12	2.2.3 Integrate	5 days	20 Jun	24 Jun	11	Sam
13	⊟ 2.3 Reports	15 days	27 Jun	15 Jul		
14	2.3.1 Design & Develop Reports	15 days	27 Jun	15 Jul	12	Sam

Figure 5 – Project Plan (Phase 1 & 2)

In some cases, entire project phases can be delegated to individuals with the skills and influence. For example, the implementation phase is delegated to Rod who is the field operations coordinator. Rod has the authority over the field staff. The project manager's job is to work closely with Rod to develop the implementation plan details, monitor the progress and assist in resolving the issues. Engaging the right people to contribute will help the project succeed.

The project plan is the communication tool you will be using with your project team to track task progress and hold task owners accountable. Here is an example of a project plan using a spreadsheet:

High Level Project Plan	Start Date	Days	May	Jun	Jul	Who
1. Discovery						
1.1 Replace Mobile Devices	02-May	3	X			Joe
1.2 Upload	05-May	2	X			Sam
1.3 Reports	09-May	5	X			Joe
2. Design & Develop						
2.1 Mobile Devices						
2.1.1 Evaluate & Select Mobile HW	16-May	5	X			Joe
2.1.2 Evaluate & Select SW	23-May	10	X			Sam
2.2 Upload						
2.2.1 Select Wireless Device	23-May	3	X			Joe
2.2.2 Program Data Upload	06-Jun	10		X		Sam
2.2.3 Integrate	20-Jun	5		X		Sam
2.3 Reports						
2.3.1 Develop Reports	27-Jun	15		X		Sam

Excel Project Plan (Phases 1 & 2)

Do not get attached to the project plan. Although, as project manager you will own the plan, make sure you are not the only person driving the plan. The secret is to collaborate on the plan with the stakeholders so that they feel like the plan belongs to them. Consider the changes they suggest, without compromising the scope, and communicate the changes you have made back to them. If the changes are not possible due to cost, schedule or resource constraints, communicate this back to the stakeholders.

Be honest about the project status, collaborate with the team and communicate often. No matter how difficult the situation, pretending things are going well will lead to project failure. Acknowledge the issue and deal with it promptly.

Identify the most important parts of the project. Understand what the critical tasks are in case you need to drop items. Which ones would you drop, and what would the consequences of dropping those pieces be? Identify and list all the tasks as you come across more details. Project planning is an iterative process. Drill down into the details with your team and then step back to aggregate the tasks into manageable work units. These can then be prioritized and sequenced in the plan.

In one project the list of tasks were growing rapidly because of the dynamics of the user and consultant meetings. Expectations were being set by the consultants to accommodate the user desires. This is a difficult situation, and as project manager you have draw the line and set priorities. One technique is to focus on short-term releases and deliver in iterative cycles. This way the users become familiar with the product, the developers better understand the technical challenges and user expectations.

	Task Name	Duration	Start	Finish	Pred	Res
15	3. Pilot and Test	10 days	18 Jul	29 Jul		
16	3.1 Pilot Site	7 days	18 Jul	26 Jul		
17	3.1.1 Prepare Site & Train	4 days	18 Jul	21 Jul	14	Rod
18	3.1.2 Test	2 days	22 Jul	25 Jul	17	Rod
19	3.1.3 Transmit	1 day	26 Jul	26 Jul	18	Rod
20	3.2 Head Office	3 days	27 Jul	29 Jul		
21	3.2.1 Data Upload	2 days	27 Jul	28 Jul	19	Joe
22	3.2.2 Reports Test	1 day	29 Jul	29 Jul	21	Joe
23	4. Impement	8 days	01 Aug	10 Aug		
24	4.1 Site 1 (Same for 2-6)	8 days	01 Aug	10 Aug		
25	Communication	1 day	01 Aug	01 Aug	22	Rod
26	Replace Mobile Devices	2 days	02 Aug	03 Aug	25	Rod
27	Transmit Data	1 day	04 Aug	04 Aug	26	Rod
28	Upload	1 day	05 Aug	05 Aug	27	Rod
29	Test Reports	2 days	08 Aug	09 Aug	28	Rod
30	Go Live	1 day	10 Aug	10 Aug	29	Rod

Figure 6 – Project Plan (Phase 3 & 4)

54

Identify Risks

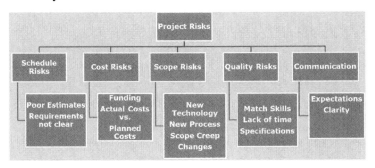

Anything that will affect the project delivery is a risk. The secret is to identify the risks and review them with the project team on a regular basis. Address and manage risks quickly. Work with the team to brainstorm solutions and develop a risk management plan.

Risk	Impact	Mitigation
Field users are reluctant to change mobile device technology	High	Involve the crew supervisors to assist with the training plan.
New mobile device software and hardware has not been tested	High	Include a pilot phase to test the devices and software.
Integration to Finance System is not defined	Low	Have the business analyst work with Finance to design the reports, specify the interfaces and identify the data that needs to be integrated.
Some sites do not have internet access	High	Investigate costs and options for the networks or alternative means of data transmission.

The risk register identifies the risk, ranks the impact to the project and provides a risk mitigation plan.

Estimate Costs

The cost has worked out to be close to the $750,000 budget. The cost picture looks good as the estimate includes a 20% contingency for unknowns.

Although the estimate looks good, it is only an initial estimate in the planning step and there may be costs uncovered as the project progresses. Additional requirements and costs are sure to be uncovered during the pilot, design, develop and implementation phases of the project.

	Unit Cost	Units	Total Cost	Comment
Hardware	3,000	150	450,000	
Software				
Purchase			50,000	Enterprise licence Fee
Customization			25,000	
Site Wireless Network				
Hardware	1,200	6	7,200	Wireless, wiring, network
Labour	2,500	5	12,500	
Data Upload				
Software integration	3,000	6	8,000	Includes testing and integration
Training			18,000	Training for 6 sites
Consultant fees			60,000	
Contingency 20%			126,140	
Total Cost			$ 756,840	

Budget and Cost Estimate

Verify and update the project plan and cost estimates after each phase. Review the updated plan and cost estimates with the project sponsors. At this stage, verify that the cost projections are still valid and make adjustments with project sponsor if required. If the budget is firm, the scope will need to be adjusted and tasks removed to fit the budget constraint. Amend the scope in the project charter with the consent of the team and ultimately the stakeholders.

Summary

In the planning phase, a lot of effort is spent on defining the tasks, estimating the work effort, identifying the resources and scheduling the work. Using the scope and project deliverables a work breakdown structure is created (WBS), which in turn is used to create the project plan.

1. Divide the project into phases, use the scope and project deliverables to decompose the work into small units creating a Work Breakdown Structure (WBS).

2. Use the WBS to develop a detailed project plan. Analyze and understand each work unit to estimate

the task duration, effort, task dependency, schedule and resources required.

3. As part of the project plan, develop a set of management plans to describe how the work will be completed and monitored for quality.

4. Develop a risk register that has a ranked list of risks and a mitigation plan for each risk.

5. Develop a project cost estimate based on the available information. Identify and document the unknowns. Identify cost checkpoints in the project to review cost assumptions. The contingency is initially high due to the project unknowns.

6. Get approval from the project sponsors on the plan, cost and risk documents prior to project execution.

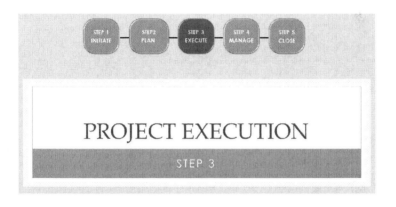

STEP 3 - EXECUTE

"Interdependent people combine their own efforts, with the efforts of others to achieve their greatest success."

Stephen Covey

The project sponsors have approved the plan and you have been given authority to proceed. There is a buzz in the organization about the new project and people are curious. Be prepared to describe clearly, the project value, scope and the identity of the sponsors. This is important communication to manage expectations. During execution, you will be communicating the project plan, working to define and build your project team, and starting the work.

Once the sponsors have formally communicated the project to the organization, hold a kickoff meeting with the project team. In this meeting, describe the project goals, objectives, scope, plan, team composition and responsibilities. Depending on the organizational culture and the project size, the kickoff meeting may be a large or informal. Large corporations may require a more formal kickoff meeting with participation from the sponsors, midsized or smaller companies may have a small information meeting to communicate the project.

Regardless of the project size, scope and value must be communicated to the company.

You need to ensure that the project sponsor identifies the project team and formally presents you as the project manager in the kickoff meeting. Project sponsors are busy people; so one approach is to provide them with a draft communication memo to send out to the organization. Be sure to invite the sponsor(s) to the kickoff meeting to say a few high level words about the project and the team. The sponsor's job is to empower the project manager, convey the project importance and set the tone for the team.

Build the Team

The availability of the project team is a critical success factor. The sponsors want to ensure project success and have the authority to help you acquire project resources, so make use of this relationship.

Based on the project plan and project deliverables, you will have good idea on the project team required. For example, the field deployment coordinator was selected because of his influence and authority over all the deployment sites and personnel. The mobile device and software selection team consists of the end users, technical team and field supervisors. Along with the technical team, it is important to give influencers the opportunity to participate in the selection process so that they can bring their experience to the table and help with project acceptance. Consumers and end users of the product must be consulted and included to ensure acceptance. Armed with this information, the scope and project plan, you will be in a good position to ask for a project team with the right mix of skills. Formalize the project team as shown in figure 7. Include the names of individuals in the team and share the project organization with the team and sponsors, so that the project roles and work expectations are clear.

You will find line managers are very protective of their staff. Managers will hold project managers accountable for their staff's utilization. Estimate resource time utilization for the duration of the project and discuss it with each manager. Get agreement on how much time their staff will spend on the project.

Compare the project team organization (figure 7) with the work breakdown structure (figure 4) and notice that the project teams will be utilized in all project phases starting from the discovery phase to the implementation phase. Not all projects will play out with the same teams. However, it is good to have some team consistency so that requirements and deliverables are clearly understood through the life of the project. The report requirements team has nothing to do with the device selection, however they do dictate what field data is required for the reports. The takeaway here is that teams will be moving in and out of the project and you as the project manager are ultimately responsible for communicating requirements across teams. Cross team meetings are good way to share requirements across tasks.

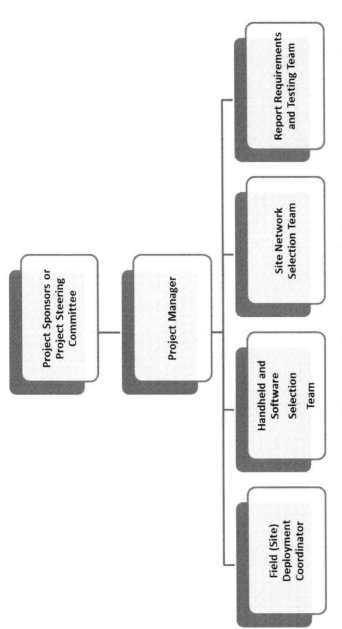

Figure 7 – Project Team Organization

Keep it Simple

Keep in mind that it is the people and the work you want to manage with aid of the project tools. Do not end up managing a project management tool or a process-diagramming tool. However, the project plan, cost estimate, risk register and dashboard, are critical tools to monitor the project and keep the team focused. Outside the formal review meetings, walk around and informally engage people. Discover likes, dislikes, investigate and address issues.

Some of the best project managers I have come across have been the ones who established great relationships with their teams. These teams in turn went the extra mile to get things done. Regardless of whether the team member works directly for the project manager or for a departmental manager you can engage individuals to assist to ensure project success.

Your influence on individuals as project manager will be greater if that person formally reports to you, and less if the team member reports to a functional manager. In the latter case, you will need to work within the constraints dictated by the functional manager and the organizational structure. If the resource is assigned to you for the duration of the project, you will have more control over the individual's time and work.

Project execution is an important phase where the actual work is being done. Before execution, time was spent on understanding the requirements, developing the project plan, acquiring the team and generally preparing to begin the project work. The project plan, dashboard, cost estimate and risk register tools are used in the executing, monitoring, controlling and closing phases of the project.

Each task's outcome in the project plan needs to be clearly understood and discussed with the task owner. Spend some time with the task owners to ensure that you, as the project manager, and the individual responsible for completing the task are clear on the effort and outcome.

Assign tasks to the individuals or teams and begin the work. Order the equipment, have your suppliers lined up, and be ready to go with the vendor contracts, purchase orders, and required company approvals.

Summary

In the executing phase, you have clarified the roles and responsibilities, communicated the project plan and lined up the resources to begin the work. Describing the project and working with the team lays the foundation for the project and establishes relationships with your project team.

1. Acquire the project team.
2. Kick off the project by communicating the project goals and objectives, scope and team.
3. Assign tasks and begin the work.

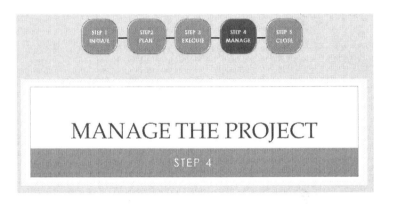

STEP 4 - MANAGE

Your job as project manager is to keep the project integrated and moving by ensuring the task owners have what they need to complete the work. The end game is to complete the tasks in the project plan and finish the project on time, on budget, and within scope while maintaining quality.

People, Meetings and Progress

One of the questions I am often asked is how frequently the meetings should be held. In general, meet the team on a regular basis and follow up as critical milestones approach. The frequencies of the meetings depend on the project size, duration, geography, the organizational culture and other factors.

Some organizations will have designated project room for the team members for the duration of the project. This especially true of software development projects. Software team leads may hold a daily meeting where quick updates are exchanged. Construction teams may hold daily work and safety meetings. Each situation is different based on the nature of project, the company culture, the industry and the organizational priority of the project. Face to face meetings help with team building and communication. However, in-person meetings are not always possible, especially if the project spans geographic boundaries.

There is no need to hold daily meetings. Much of the communication can be done via phone calls, conversations in the hallway and via emails. I expect people to be self-accountable, to be clear on their tasks and to report progress. Depending on the project size, a weekly meeting or conference call to review the plan is a good way to keep the team focused, track progress and plan work for the next week. In general, develop a close working relationship with everyone involved in the project. Send the project sponsors a periodic dashboard update with a brief narrative on what was accomplished, activities planned for the next month, budget status and issues.

The meetings can be divided into project teams, such as software design, mobile device selection, site wireless installation, and training. The monitor and control meetings cover the following areas:

SPARTAN PROJECT MANAGEMENT

1) Clarify work and encourage self-accountability.

2) Monitor project status and individual work progress.

3) Ensure the work is within the defined scope.

4) Verify the requirements are being met.

5) Validate the quality of the deliverables and address if there are quality issues.

6) Plan work and activities for the next period.

7) Manage and address resource scheduling.

8) Review issues and develop approaches to address those issues and risks.

9) Report on the project progress and status.

10) Communicate across teams.

11) Integrate and coordinate work and teams.

12) Review and update the relevant sections of the project plan and the dashboard.

13) Ensure that contracts meet quality expectations.

14) Monitor and manage costs, time and risks

Review the dashboard and track the progress with the team. The dashboard will show progress at a high level and will help encourage and motivate the project team.

Informal and hallway meetings are a good way to track progress and uncover issues, as long as you are not

73

overbearing or micro managing. Trust people and make sure they understand the deliverables for their assigned tasks. Keep in mind, hallway interactions are no substitute for formal meetings to review and follow up on the project plan. Monitor their performance, but at the same time, empower individuals to work within their levels of expertise.

Projects can have many complexities; some apparent, some invisible and others unknown. You need to be prepared best you can and be able to dynamically adjust to new situations. Knowing the project scope well will help you respond to project changes. In most cases, out of scope requests need to be put aside, as they will have an impact on the schedule, cost and resources.

Include some members of the team to present the results to the sponsors with the updated plan when possible. Share the stage, share the victories and your team will support you. The biggest mistake is to stand alone and take all the glory, as it will lead to resentment, and possibly project sabotage. Review and update the dashboard with the stakeholders and sponsors.

As the project manager, you have the big picture of how the project pieces fit together from the field to headquarters. Be sure that you understand the interconnectivity of the deployment logistics, geographic locations, and various stakeholders.

It is your job, as the big picture person, to ensure all the parts integrate into the whole. The goal is to replace aging mobile device technology with newer more cost effective technology and in the process you will improve the data collection and reporting back to head office. This project will improve equipment service, uptime, safety and cost. However, more importantly that the company depends on the equipment productivity for its business and the cost of equipment failure is high. Understand that there may be issues due to problems with mobile device adoption, network failures and the integration of the new data into the financial systems. As project manager, you need to ensure that all the parts are integrated and tested well before going live with the new system.

The selected mobile devices must work well with the mobile device software. These two tasks cannot be developed in isolation or by separate teams. Identify task dependencies and orchestrate collaboration and communication between teams. Ensure the training meets these needs and is of the highest quality.

The field personnel need training and the devices and software must be easy for the field staff to use. The devices must also have wireless capability to transmit the data. The inventory and financial systems need to be configured and ready to consume the enhanced equipment data. Follow up on all dependent project tasks such as acquiring wireless capable devices, developing excellent training, and preparing the inventory and financial systems.

Engage the Team

Do not work in isolation. Work with the resources and end users to manage the plan. There will be subject matter experts and stakeholders to assist you, ask for help, as nobody expects you to be an expert in all areas. However, they do expect you to manage the project deliverables. For each major task category, you need to know how much is done, how much work is left, what issues exist, and how much of the budget has been used.

In addition, you will need information to report to the sponsors on the project status. If you are on top of the plan and are aware of the issues, it will demonstrate that you are in control. The key is to remain objective, know the project plan status at all times, be honest and address the issues to gain the support and respect of the stakeholders.

Stakeholders are people directly or indirectly impacted by the project. Treat them as you would your customers because ultimately they will accept or reject the project. In the example the handheld users are important stakeholders and we know that they are concerned about using the new devices. By assigning the field supervisor to ensure success, risk has been mitigated.

Compare the project performance against the project management plan. There may be chaotic times during the project, where things break and generally appear to be in crisis. Take time to step back and look at how these issues fit into the grand scheme of things by using the dashboard. Bring the team together and show them where the current issues fit in the plan. Next, drill into the issues and brainstorm ideas on how to resolve the issues. This will be the leadership, which will lift the team from crisis to solution oriented thinking. Your job will be to leverage the team expertise and bring calmness by stepping back and focusing on the big picture.

One of the problems is that projects take on a life of their own. By this, I mean projects lose sight or their original goals and objectives. This is one of the key reasons for cost and time overruns resulting in project failure. To avoid this situation, briefly review the goals and objectives at the beginning of each meeting. This information is already in the project dashboard, so it is easy to access during the meeting. After a few meetings, people will say that they know this already but it sets the tone for the rest of the meeting to focus on the agreed charter. The charter is what the project sponsor agreed to.

Actively managed at this stage are the people, tasks, costs and risks. Project teams are engaged and there is there is a high level of project activity. Ensure that tasks are completed and people are engaged in delivering scheduled tasks. Use the project plan to review progress with the task owners, determine start dates, expected completion dates and percentage completion of each task. Empower them and help them resolve issues. Encourage ownership of tasks and self-accountability.

Refine the Project Plan

By the time you reach the implementation phase, the mobile devices, software, upload process and reports have been developed and tested. User acceptance and the field-training plan have been refined. The project team is now aware of what it will take to deploy these units to production. Update the project plan based on the information you know and refine it as you get more information.

Watch the Costs

The original planned cost is referred to as the cost baseline or budget. Monitor the cost estimates at a detail level and at total level. Compare the cost utilization against project completion for each cost component. In this example, the expenditure to date is broken down by project phase.

	Unit Cost	Units	Total Cost	Discovery	Design & Develop	Pilot & Test	Implement	Total Utilized
Mobile Device Hardware	3,000	150	450,000		6,000	42,000		48,000
Software								-
Licence Fee			50,000					
Customization			25,000	-	2,000	8,000	-	10,000
Site Wireless Network								-
Hardware	1,200	6	7,200		1,200			1,200
Labour	2,500	5	12,500		500	2,000		2,500
Data Upload								-
Software integration			8,000			3,000		3,000
Training	3,000	6	18,000		500	2,000		2,500
Consultant fees			60,000	2,000	8,000	5,000		15,000
Contingency 20%			126,140					-
Total Cost			756,840	2,000	18,200	62,000	0	82,200

Budget vs. Completion	Planned	Actual Budget Used	Percent Budget Used	Percent Project Complete
	750,000	82,200	11%	15%

At the minimum, track and compare each cost line item and compare it to the related project deliverable. For example, at the summary level 15% of the project is complete and 11% of the funds have been spent. This is generally a good indicator but it can be deceiving. For example, a deeper investigation reveals that the project has completed the initial investigation phase, and is now entering the design and develop phase. A large amount has been spent ($48,000) on mobile devices in the pilot and test phase. The 16 units purchased may not pass the pilot test, in which case the funds would be wasted. A decision to purchase fewer units or rent units for the pilot phase may be a better approach. The project manager will be required to make project decisions based on cost constraints. Decisions such as testing fewer units or renting mobile device units will need to be balanced against the project risks and project plan. Costs need to monitored and managed throughout the project.

Cost management is a large topic and there are many aspects to cost control and management, only the basics are covered here. Another way to manage costs is to break down the budgets and estimates by phase. Each line item would have a budget and "cost to date" column for every phase (discovery, design and develop, pilot and test, implement). This method permits costs to be compared with percent complete for each phase.

Some companies may have project accounting systems in which case you will need to break down the project by cost codes as required by the finance department. Other companies will also track resource utilization and may have accounting requirements that dictate how the budget and costs tracked. Regardless of the system, keep a record of the allocated funds and costs to date at all times. Compare the expenditures against the budget and project completion to monitor and manage project related costs. To manage the cost risk, monitor how much work is remaining relative to the remaining funds.

Manage the Risks

In the monitoring and controlling phase, you will have better information on the project risks. In the example, the risk register has been updated with new information; it shows risks are actively being managed.

Risk Register	Impact	Mitigation
Field users are reluctant to change mobile device technology	Low	Downgraded to a low, as field supervisors are now part of the project team. The field supervisor have committed to assist with the training and implementation of the mobile devices
New mobile device software and hardware has not been tested	Low	Conducted site visits to other companies who are using this technology and the risk has been downgraded to a low based on the findings.
Integration to Finance System is not defined	Low	Have the business analyst work with Finance team to design the reports, specify the interfaces and identify the data that needs to be integrated. - TBD
Some sites do not have internet access	High	Investigate costs and options for the networks or alternative means of data transmission.
Cost	Med	Full costs of the project, support and customization are still not clear. Update cost information from the pilot phase.

Innovation

During the project, new ideas on better ways to complete the tasks will be presented. Accept and approve valuable ideas if they do not add to scope or cost. The Spartan way is to embrace innovation without adding unnecessary bells and whistles. Projects and teams are dynamic and decisions are continuously made within the constraints of scope, cost and time. Make sure that the passenger plane does not mutate into an unusable fighter jet. Keep true to the core requirements in the project charter.

Summary

As project manager, you are constrained by time, budget and resources. You may find yourself pressured to add features and work to the project. You need to stick to the constraints of the plan as well as keep a healthy working relationship with the stakeholders and sponsors. Communicate often and advise the stakeholders that changes are not possible without impacting cost, quality or schedules. Keep the good ideas around for future consideration or if the pressure is too great, engage the project team and raise the proposed scope change with project sponsors if necessary. Any change in scope will affect the schedule, cost or resource requirements. The project plan, dashboard, cost and risk register tools are used to monitor and control the project.

Working with teams and individuals to monitor and action project tasks is a key activity in this step.

1. Monitor, manage and update the project plan with the team. Review the work completed, plan the work ahead and verify individuals are completing the work.

2. Monitor costs and make decisions related to budget utilization with the team.

3. Update and follow up on the risks.

4. Ensure that the quality of the work is up to standard.

5. Ensure all the work is within the defined scope.

6. Empower individuals and encourage self-accountability.

STEP 5 – TRANSITION & CLOSE

"The world is round and the place which may seem like the end may also be the beginning."
Ivy Baker Priest

Project closure is difficult to achieve without a smooth transition to operations. The project team must ensure that operations have the training and support they need to operate the mobile devices. In our case, a three-month transition period was built into the project plan and the field supervisors were part of the project team. Once the transition to operations is complete, you can begin the process of closing the project. The key stakeholders must approve the handoff.

Since that you have been reviewing the dashboard from the beginning, the project team, the project stakeholders and the sponsors are clear on what project closure means. Everybody is on the same page because the closure document has been a working dashboard for the team. Project closure is an iterative process, since there might be some items that are not accepted. You will need to address these items before closure or defer them as a future enhancement. The dashboard will help close the gap to ensure project acceptance. Using the dashboard ensures that the end vision as described in the project charter has been delivered.

The Success Story

As Project Manager, you have used the right tools and techniques to deliver a success story.

Here is an example of a narrative to accompany the project closure dashboard:

The project was delivered under budget as planned within the specified time frame; contingency funds were utilized due to weather related site closures that resulted in rescheduling and increased training costs. Initial pilot tests failed, which also required funds from the contingency pool.

Overall, the field supervisors are happy with the new devices and all six sites are in production with the new devices and technology. All field supervisors have signed off on the new mobile devices. The field data is seamlessly transmitted to head office and integrated into both the financial and inventory systems. Both the finance and inventory teams are using the field data and reports and have confirmed that their stated requirements have been met.

The report shows that all the project critical success factors have been met and the project is now complete. The project team has put in place support procedures and the sites have been live with the new system for 3 months.

Confirm that the project delivered the value stated in the project charter. For example, verify that the business goals and objectives to improve data quality, device reliability and support are accepted. The critical success factors were achieved the project deliverables were completed. This is implicit in the acceptance of the project closure dashboard.

The purpose of the closure phase is to get agreement from the project sponsors and stakeholders that the project is closed and complete. The dashboard is a tool to help you get agreement across the board. Upon agreement, declare the project closed and celebrate with the project team.

Collect and Archive Lessons

Save information on cost estimates and actual costs to use as guidelines in future projects. Learn from your projects and archive all the project documents including the WBS. Save historical information on actual costs and duration of tasks to help you with estimates in future projects.

On completion collect and document information on what worked well and what did not. Capture information on future improvements. Do this while the project information is still fresh. Summarize these findings and review them with the team as a final and formal closure step. A project has a beginning and an end and the project must end with this step.

Project Closure dashboard	Description	Accepted
Project Definitions and Scope	Replace the aging mobile devices in 6 field offices with new mobile devices. Improve the process of uploading the mobile device data to head office. Load the mobile device data into the enterprise financial and inventory systems. Develop Reports.	Project was delivered with the specified scope.
Business Goals and Objectives	• To improve the uptime, safety, service and life of the field equipment (trucks, cranes, tractors). • To reduce the cost and time lost to problems with mobile data collection devices in the field. • Collect more relevant data to the business and improve the data quality. • Eliminate the support risk and cost of old technology	Accepted Accepted Accepted Accepted
Critical Success Factors	• Seamless replacement of devices with no disruption to current business operations. • Ease of use of the mobile devices and adoption by field personnel • Meet or exceed existing functionality	Accepted, although there were some issues Accepted Accepted Has significantly added value to the business
Project Deliverables	• Replace mobile devices with new models • Improve equipment data collection and processes • Train field personnel • Implement site wireless infrastructure • Transmit mobile device data to head office • Upload data to the inventory and finance systems • Improve financial and field inventory reporting	Complete Complete Complete Complete Works Works Accepted
Project Schedule	• As per project plan	Accepted and delivered on schedule

93

Field Office	Mobile devices Deployed	Training Complete	Wireless Installed	Site Operational	Comment
Site 1	Yes	Yes	Yes	Yes	
Site 2	Yes	Yes	Yes	Yes	
Site 3	Yes	Yes	Yes	Yes	
Site 4	Yes	Yes	Yes	Yes	
Site 5	Yes	Yes	No	Yes	No wireless, USB transfer
Site 6	Yes	Yes	Yes	Yes	

Key Project Tasks	Complete	Comment
Devices Selected	Yes	Contract was awarded to the vendor with the best support, warranty and replacement plan.
Software Selected	Yes	
Software Customized	Yes	Vendor support agreements need to be signed off
Data Fields Added	Yes	
Field Data Collected	Yes	
Inventory Report X	Yes	
Inventory Report Y	Yes	
Financial Report A	Yes	
Financial Report B	No	Project Decision – Not completed since the field data could not be integrated into the Finance system. Finance decided to defer this enhancement for the future. The Finance system requires an upgrade which is out of scope.

Budget vs. Completion	Planned	Actual Budget Used	Percent Budget Used	Percent Project Complete
	750,000	710,000	95%	100%

THE PROJECT CHECKLIST

Along this journey, you have earned credibility as project manager by developing, managing and communicating the plan. This guide provides you with a project management framework to build on. It gives you the core principals and tools to initiate, plan, execute, manage and close a project. The checklist table summarizes the five steps and key templates required to manage a project.

At the initiation phase, you worked with the project sponsors to define the scope, identify the project team, and develop the project charter and the dashboard. During the planning phase, the project tasks were broken down into smaller workable tasks to develop the project plan complete with the schedule and associated resources. Next, during the project execution and the managing step you used the project plan and dashboard to monitor progress, schedule work, hold individuals to task and communicate the project status to the team and stakeholders. Finally, as the project nears completion, use the dashboard to close the project.

Step	Templates	Create	Update	Use
1. Initiating Get approval	Project Charter Dashboard	X X		
2. Planning Build plan, budget tracking tool, risk management tool	Project Charter Dashboard Work Breakdown Structure Project Plan Cost Register Risk Register	 X X X X		X X
3. Executing Build team, communicate project start	Project Charter Dashboard Project Plan Cost Register Risk Register		 X X	X X X
4. Manage Manage plan, monitor and control, schedule, cost and risk	Project Charter Dashboard Project Plan Cost Register Risk Register		 X X X X	X X X X X
5. Close Handover project to daily operations by putting contracts and support in place	Project Charter Project Plan Dashboard Cost Register Risk Register		 X X	X X X X X

Embedded in this guide, I presented communication techniques and conveyed some concepts on emotional intelligence. Like a true Spartan you were clear on your objectives, focused on the core requirements and empowered team members to be self-accountable. You provided clear leadership based on a well-defined scope, charter and dashboard.

On completion of this guide, you now have an understanding of the entire project process with some invaluable templates and techniques that can be applied to any project you undertake. I encourage you to apply these templates and the five steps in your next project.

Like a hero's journey, a project is a quest to complete the mission. The journey may not be easy but it is rewarding to complete.

CREATIVITY IN PROJECTS

"You are told the world is the way it is"
Steve Jobs

Steve Jobs said in an interview, "When you grow up you are told the world is the way it is" He said this because he never accepted the way things were and thus pushed his team and the product for excellence. Steve Jobs revolutionized the music industry with the iPod and iTunes; he revolutionized mobile technology with the iPhone and the iPad and animated films with Toy Story. He was squeezed out of Apple and came back to make it the company it is today. He never accepted failure; he learned from his experiences and persisted.

Although the tone in this book has been to monitor and control scope and change, my training as a software engineer is to build and learn from short iterative cycles. This is approach is inherently creative.

So what does this all have to do with creativity? Lets define it first. <u>Creativity</u> is the capacity to make connections, explore and develop interesting work. The <u>creative process</u> is how we get from idea to product using creativity.

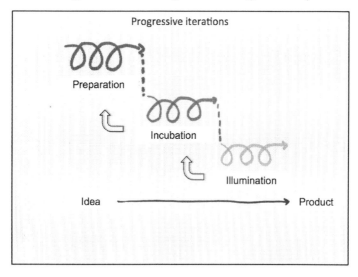

There are three key iterative stages in the creative process. These are preparation, incubation and illumination. Having informal team meetings where people are encouraged to share ideas improve the process and product in short iterative cycles. There are many approaches such as agile and scrum meetings that foster this. As always complete short-term cycles while keeping the end goal and time line in mind. This is just the way business projects work. The sponsors want results within the time and cost constraints.

Walt Disney got the idea to animate cartoons on films at the age of 13, this idea incubated with him for many years before he applied it. The first time he started his animation studio he lost it all because of lack of experience. He learned from his failures and started from scratch with a character called Mickey Mouse. The rest is history. Both Disney and Jobs learned from the experiences and failures. Discussing openly what worked well and what did not is key to embracing continuous improvement.

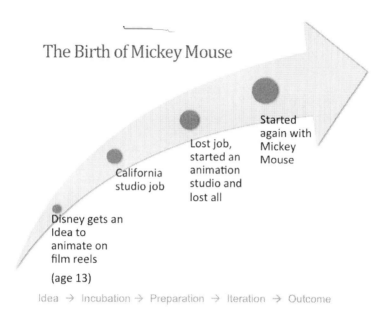

The Birth of Mickey Mouse

Started again with Mickey Mouse

Lost job, started an animation studio and lost all

California studio job

Disney gets an Idea to animate on film reels

(age 13)

Idea → Incubation → Preparation → Iteration → Outcome

Depending on your project scope and timeframe, you and your team will incubate many ideas before someone hits that eureka moment and the idea can be applied. This pattern happens over and over in software development as teams get more proficient and understand customer needs better. These incubated ideas are progressively incorporated into the product and process within the constraints of time, quality, scope and cost.

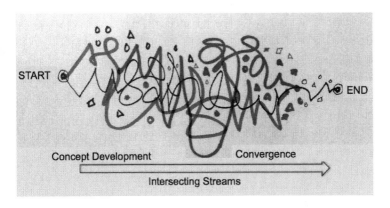

Concept Development   Convergence

Intersecting Streams

When you start a project there will be many ideas and concepts. These ideas intersect and converge as the product matures. During this time the team and stakeholders should be coming to a common understanding of what the end product will look like. It is your job as project manager to facilitate a common understanding.

For example in the field data collection project, the field tablets were replaced, new data collection software was introduced and a new process to update the data into the central database was introduced. One of the biggest challenges was that the staff resisted the change because the new tablets and software were not tested and perceived as incapable. The challenge for the project manager is not only to ensure credible products and processes are in place but to get corporation from the technical teams, business owners and end users.

As the project progresses you will come across technical, resource, scope and time constraints. The convergence period is also an opportunity to engage the stakeholders and get them to test drive the product. As they get familiar with the product they will gain an understanding and appreciation of what it can do. No doubt you will get many suggestions and ideas, embrace them and consider them for future iterations if possible.

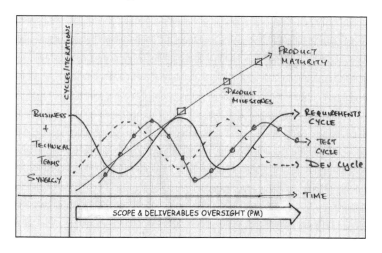

The diagram shows how product maturity relates to the requirements, test and development cycle.

The chart shows how requirement cycles interlace with development and testing cycles across business and technical teams while the PM keeps the line of sight on deliverables and overall scope. The synergy across teams happens throughout these cycles.

Regardless of the size or type of the project, if you want quality then having product iterations and reviews is key. The project team is continuously evolving and learning from each other. As project manager you must facilitate this, after all you have a team of experts to leverage.

PROJECT MANAGEMENT AS A STORY

Background

This section is based on scenarios from my graphic novel *The Cheese in Between*. It is story about Max the project manager and his journey to complete his project.

There are many things that happen behind the scenes in the office, there are complex characters and departments that have their own priorities. People may also have hidden agendas and block the project for various reasons such as fear of job loss or new technology. There are also rumours that impact the how the project is seen, referred to project optics. In the formal sense the graphic novel covers a project from initiation to completion, but it's not just a story about the project. It's about the people and the project is playing in the background. It is about Max on a journey to complete his project.

The diagram shows a project manager's journey, based on Joseph Campbell's Hero's Journey. The ordinary world is the as-is situation and the treasure is the end result.

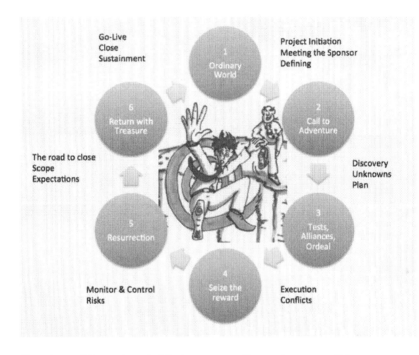

Starting with project initiation or a call to adventure, Max begins his journey. He starts with a discovery phase where he builds relationships and comes to terms with his ordeal (scope.) He seizes the opportunity and begins his quest with a discovery of his new world. It's a hard journey but in the end he is rewarded with a successful project. In the graphic novel awkward scenarios are presented to Max. In the previous picture his boss, Mr. Lee, is flinging Max into user land. As a project manager you will find yourself in new environments that you will need to discover and explore. Adapting to these environments is key as you learn about the business processes, the company culture and the teams you work with.

Project Rhythm

Projects have rhythm, ebbs and flows. Everything is connected like external markets, company share prices, departmental politics and people's behaviours. Scarcity creates competition and in times of abundance the atmosphere is more forgiving. Just like natural eco systems, more food brings more rabbits; more rabbits in turn bring more predators. Money for projects bring in vendors, consultants and often technology the organization may not be prepared for. More work, scope and money may come your way and needs to be closely monitored and managed.

In the graphic novel, there is a mandate from the board to reduce costs and the executives spring into action. The VP of Technology instructs the CIO to reduce costs, which spawns an initiative to replace the old and expensive legacy call center system. This is an opportunity to modernize with mobile technology and fit into the "green" initiative. Mega Corp wants to be seen as an environmentally friendly company. "Go-Green, Go-Mobile" becomes the brand and battle cry for the project. It is sexy because it is green and mobile, but lacks substance because there is no direct business benefit and not quantifiable.

Mr. Lee provides Max with a vague set of guidelines, which include: (1) reduce costs, (2) replace the legacy call center system, (3) go green, and (3) go mobile.

That is all the guidance Max gets and so he struggles to define the goals and objectives.

In fact Mr. Lee has no idea himself, so when confronted he pushes Max against the wall commands him to "Just Do It." As project manager it is critical you develop a clear understanding of the goals and objectives and get written agreement. This agreement is formalized in the project charter.

In *The Cheese in Between*, Max tries to clarify the project goals and uncover the risks but fails. Thus the seed for project disaster is sowed early since the goals and objectives are vague and the risks were not articulated. What I am saying is you need to cover yourself and your professional reputation. Be true to the client and the sponsor; above all be true to yourself.

Mr. Lee, a busy middle manager does not have the foresight to help Max out. Mr. Lee is a survivor and he is well connected in the company. He is the strategic guy while Max is the tactical guy who makes it happen. This is where the strategic and tactical worlds collide because of all the grey areas in between.

The project strategy is broad and the goals and objectives cannot be clearly articulated by Max. The intent and the spirit of the project get lost in translation from the board, to Mr. Lee to Max and ultimately the project team.

The project cost is huge coming in at seven million dollars, but less than ten percent of the overall company cost reduction initiative of a hundred million dollars. Therefore the stage is set for the project to spawn a life of its own, deserving only monthly high level steering committee meetings. Here is where the work begins in managing expectations, scope and cost.

On Project Launch and Branding

Mr. Lee is eager to get Mega Corp to buy into his project. So the "Go-Green, Go-Mobile" branding is born. This tag line gives the project company wide visibility and importance because it is tied into the chairman's mandate to reduce costs.

A company wide launch party is held celebrating the brand and announcing the project followed by a project kick off. The project kick off does not go so well as Max is flung to users who do not want to change.

Office Culture and Characters

Max is yanked out his help desk cubicle and catapulted into the project manager position. He has no formal project management training or experience, but he is smart, has a good heart and popular. Max is new and does not carry scars from previous projects. People in the company like him. Mr. Lee knows this and exploits his popularity by putting him in charge of a company critical project.

Jenny wants to be project manager. This is established early in the graphic novel. During the course of the story I establish and reinforce her jealousy and devious nature. Her plan is to take over as project manager by discrediting Max and the project. Jenny is the communications officer and the antagonist in the story.

Kumar on the other hand, lives for technology. He loves technology, eats it and breathes it. He is a typical developer next door. I used to be a software developer and loved to code and see my work used by customers or sometimes just used by me.

Kumar emerges as the technical lead due to his knowledge and the team respects his word. So when he confronts project manager over the development approach and time estimates his team back him up.

Humans crave for identity; they form groups and align themselves to groups. The company rhythm creates an environment and project becomes a goal. People rally and align themselves around a goal with the right leadership.

However like some families, companies and projects can get dysfunctional. This occurs when there is struggle for power in the leadership, a vacuum created by a departing manager or by interdepartmental conflicts.

Tribal Cultures

I exaggerate tribal cultures by creating a user culture in a make believe eco system at Mega Corp. One of the users I worked with, a subject matter expert often referred to users as having "tribal knowledge." I explored and exploited this tribal concept. This is not far from the truth in most organizations.

In corporate environments departments operate in silos as they typically have their own operations and business drivers. I provided Max with a subject matter expert to help him in his discovery of user world. Business analysts, developers and project managers are often thrown into business areas that are foreign to them. With them they take analytical tools and techniques to understand the business. They look for people to help them understand and discover this new business.

Planning and Estimating

When the initial excitement of project announcement and initiation is over, Max begins to plan and estimate the schedule and cost.

The next cartoon depicts an unconcerned Mr. Lee dropping the burden of the project estimate on Max. Mr. Lee is relaxed with his feet on his desk, while Max struggles with how to determine a realistic estimate. Max is overwhelmed and because there are so many unknowns at this stage. I think, Max should be using the risk management template and discussing the risks with his team and stakeholders.

A project is organic; it is in fact living and breathing entity. It changes form and shape due to budgets, technical limitations, time, people, office politics and company priorities. Project scope agreements are often forgotten and new deliverables are added such as demo apps. In the graphic novel, Mr. Lee gets Kumar to show a tablet app to Jasmine without Max's knowledge. This adds scope, complexity and time to the project. The expectations have been set and now Max needs to manage the expectations or ask for more time and money to include the tablets in the scope.

Stages of Stress

Both Max and Jenny are early in their careers and looking to prove themselves, which contributes to stress. Kumar is very much in the now, all he thinks about is the next code snippet to write. The reality is that need for recognition, ambition and ego all contribute to stress and tense environments.

The initiation and planning stage are the honeymoon period and the stress is light. The project tempo picks up during the execution phase and gets higher in monitor and control phase. This where conflicts occur around requirements, priorities, design, technology, schedules, people and resources. For example Max ends up in a conflict with Kumar over the quality of the requirements and the estimated development time. He does a reality check on the plan, which results in confronting Mr. Lee for more time. Conflict occurs because the team is working within the constraints of time, technology, scope and cost.

The monitor and control phase is the second most stressful period. The most stressful time for the project team is the time leading up to going live with the new system. This is where fear and anxiety come into play because this is when the rubber hits the road. The new system is critical to the department operations and success. The old system must be replaced and the new one must perform so the stakes are high. In the closing phase, Mr. Sharp the consultant takes this as an opportunity to sell a hosted cloud solution. In desperation Mr. Lee agrees to the utopian vision of a cloud hosted solution.

The above cartoon panel shows a typical example of adding more complexity to the project. In this scenario, it's a desperate attempt to speed up the project by moving the infrastructure to the cloud. Cloud hosting comes with its own share or requirements such as integrations with the existing internal infrastructure, support and potential performance issues. Now, these can all be managed but it will require time, expertise and money.

Projects as a Mission

When you commit to a project, you want to succeed. So you sell a vision and invest both your time and the team's time into project. You become vested in the situation and the environment like an actor in a drama.

Power, prestige, ego, recognition and just plain old primitive human emotions manifest themselves on the corporate stage. This is where Jenny makes a play by snooping for information, calling for an audit.

Mega Corp is a sandbox and microcosm of society; Mr. Lee gets his hands on mobile devices that provide information on employee activities, conversations and geo-locations both during work and off hours. Mr. Lee knows information is power and he can use the information. Max struggles with this, but keeps going as the tactical project manager.

Orchestrated information blurts on social networks have been used to oust governments for better or worse. Information blurts become information waves and waves turn into movements. Regular update meetings also help you manage communication.

Jenny knows she has control as communication officer; she uses her personal networks, social media, and office blog in her attempt to take over as project manager.

In closing, a project lives as part of an office ecosystem and the players perform both on stage and behind the scenes to drive agendas. This section was not only about the theory behind the graphic novel, but also a way to speak candidly about real life scenarios we have all been in. It is not peppered with fancy language such as emotional intelligence, human resource management or communications.

A graphic novel without an antagonist, a battle and a quest to find the treasure would have been boring; similarly a project without challenges would also be boring. Real projects have challenges and constraints, so plan ahead for issues and work through the ones you come across with your team. As the diagram below shows you will be working with multiple interest groups, ranging from managers, to technical teams to end users.

As a project manager it is important to be inclusive, transparent and to gain trust by being open and honest. Communication and building relationships are important skills to hone.

Appendix A – Gems

Key elements of project success

1. A responsive and engaged Steering Committee. They are the type who take ownership of the project and help with risks. Risks related to schedule, scope, cost, quality and stakeholder satisfaction.

2. Deep engagement by the business users. Engaging the users helps with project satisfaction.

3. Managing scope is another key success factor. On one project I was concerned about time and cost due to the hundreds of pages of requirements. We lost sight of the big picture. In fact the original creators of the requirements had left the project and there was no continuity in the understanding of the requirements. I worked with the stakeholders on zeroing in on the product critical success factors. I asked the developers for estimates and their sense of complexity. Based on these elements and business priorities we came to an agreement on release 1, the go-live release.

4. Quality assurance, testing and user training are the pillars of success. Testing real life scenarios and exception scenarios are essential to validating functionality and business rules. User acceptance test cycles and user training not only uncover problems before deployment but also acclimatize the business users to the new system, an essential component of change management.

5. The people involved in the sub-projects and tasks such as data conversion, setting up the infrastructure (web servers, app servers, integrations, databases) are unsung heroes. Respect and leverage their expertise.

6. The product architecture selected must be adaptable, that is it must have the ability to change. An example is to use technology that can isolate components such as the UI,

business rules and data. Spend time on getting the design right and incorporate industry best practices.

7. Friendship, respect and open communication are key to resolving issues. Conflicts typically revolve around requirements, quality and development time.

Many of these project success factors existed in my other projects. In all projects, I was fortunate to have the backing of the management, great technical teams, stakeholder participation and a strong business case. As project manager a large percentage of my time was spent on communication, relationship building, reporting, and facilitating.

Project Management Tip

Focus on communication with the team and stakeholders. Encourage and facilitate collaboration between the developers, business analysts, QA and the stakeholders. Catch issues early and establish the ground rules of collaboration.

Benefits of using the five Steps and Templates

1. Avoid cost overruns by managing risks and tasks

2. Develop realistic schedules

3. Meet expectations by using the Charter & Dashboard

4. Clarify work using the project plan with clear work assignments

5. Avoid overbuilding by managing scope

6. Avoid the "never-ending" project syndrome by managing scope and focusing in the End

7. Clarify ambiguous projects by defining the work & outcomes

8. Actively monitor and manage risks

Role of a Project Manager

1. Defines, plans and delivers the project

2. Provides leadership

3. Engages the team to achieve the desired outcome

4. Introduces incremental benefits

5. Makes sure that all the parts integrate

6. Is the big picture person

7. Is ultimately accountable to the project sponsor

Some Reasons Why Projects Fail

1. Cost overruns

2. Unrealistic schedules

3. Does not meet expectations

4. Project team is not clear on what to do

5. Not keeping true to the core business needs and requirements (building a Ferrari for logging work)

6. The perpetual project

7. Projects may be ambiguous

8. PM has responsibility but not the authority

9. Risks are not managed

A Typical Project Has:

1. People (sponsors, stakeholders, vendors)

2. One or more geographic locations

3. Introduction of a new process, service or product

4. Has defined outcomes (product, process or service)

5. Constraints (time, money, resources, scope)

6. A return on investment (ROI) for the company

Handling Project Unknowns

- Actively manage risks
    - There will be incidents
    - Brainstorm solutions with the team (utilize best practices & SOP's)
    - Ideally the project has contingencies built into the plan (cost, time, scope)
- Project value needs to be periodically assessed
    - When cost exceeds value, discuss project termination and options with the team and the sponsor. Make a decision with the sponsor.
- Refine the project plan
    - Look for opportunities without comprising core company values such as safety and quality
    - Know that changing one item (scope, schedule or cost) will have a direct impact on the other two.
    - Separate the nice to haves from the must haves
    - Apply or keep good ideas for future enhancements

Keeping Your Project Spartan

Do everything necessary to get the job done, with no extra frills, bells or whistles.

- The vision, goals, objectives, scope and deliverables are developed with the sponsors or management team

- Project value is captured at the beginning and confirmed at the end

- Connect the End (objective) and the Means (the project steps and cost)

- Work closely with the project sponsor to ensure the End is still the focus of the project.

Avoid situations where projects take on a life of their own

- Use the Project Charter to reiterate the End

- Keep the team focused on the Charter

Although PM's hold resources accountable - empower team members to:

- Run with the plan

- Be self accountable

- Take responsibility for achieving results

- Ask for help

Project Handoff on Close

- Effective handoff should be part of the project closure

- Effectively capture the benefits

- Review and remind everyone of the agreed End vision

Summary 5 Project Steps

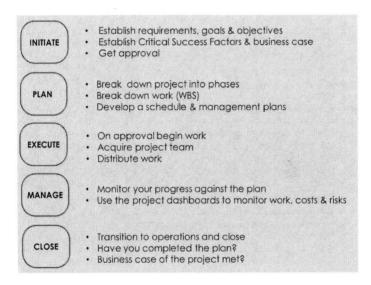

Project Initiation

- Start with the END in mind

- Describe what the project looks like on completion

- Get this END definition from the project sponsor

During the initiation phase:

- Information is gathered on the project
- Goals and objectives are defined
- Scope is defined
- Understand budget constraints
- Understand the business value
- Work with the project sponsor

The project manager is investigating and discovering more about the project, the business requirements and the company culture.

Project Plan Purpose

1. To meet the goals and objectives by completing the defined work
2. Working document to achieve an the End result by:
   - Measuring work progress
   - Monitoring work
   - Managing and controlling work

Project Plan Phase

- Estimate work (WBS)
- Sequence tasks

- Identify resources
- Develop a project plan
- Estimate cost
- Develop a risk register

Use the Project Plan to:

1. Follow the project plan
2. Clarify work and encourage self-accountability.
3. Verify the requirements are being met.
4. Validate the quality of the deliverables and address if there are quality issues.
5. Plan work and activities for the next period.
6. Manage and address resource scheduling.

Manage Phase

1. Review issues and develop approaches to address issues and risks.
   - Keep communication lines open
   - Brainstorm solutions with experts and the team
2. Monitor and control the project.
   - Review work progress against the plan
   - Actively monitor and manage costs, time and risks

- Review and update the project plan and the dashboard.
- Report progress to the sponsor, team and stakeholders
- Ensure that contracts are upheld to the quality expectations, based on service level agreements

Manage Tools

1. Project Dashboard
2. Project Plan
3. Scope
4. Risk Register
5. Cost Register

Project Closure

Has the "End" been achieved?

- Goals and objectives met?
- Has the original business case been reviewed?
- Use the dashboard to close the project
- Project transition and handoff to operations
- Iterative process until acceptance

Appendix B – Templates

PROJECT CHARTER

Project Charter (1/2)	Description
Scope	
Business Goals and Objectives	
Project Approach	
Assumptions	
Critical Success Factors	

Project Charter (2/2)	Description
Project Deliverables	
Project Team and Responsibilities	
Project Budget	
Initial Risk Analysis and Assessment	
Project Schedule	

DASHBOARDS

Project Dashboard	Description	Accepted
Project Definitions and Scope		
Business Goals and Objectives		
Critical Success Factors		
Project Deliverables		
Project Schedule		

Progress Dashboard					

Key Task Dashboard	Complete	Comment

Deliverables Dashboard	Complete	Comment

Budget vs. Completion Dashboard	Planned	Actual Budget Used	Percent Budget Used	Percent Project Complete

142

RISK REGISTER

Risk Register	Impact	Mitigation

PROJECT PLAN

Phase	Start Date	Days	May	Jun	Jul	Who	Status

COST REGISTER

Project Phase	Total Cost	Used	Remaining	% Funds Used	% Project Complete	Comment
Total Cost						

PROJECT TEAM

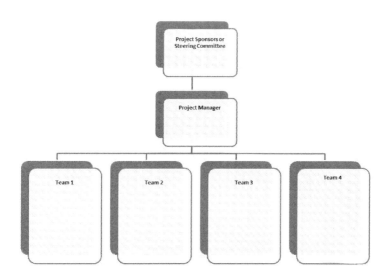

WORK BREAKDOWN STUCTURE (WBS)

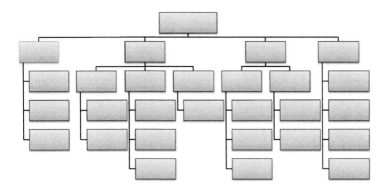

Break down the project into phases and list them in the second level boxes. Break each phase into sub-phases or tasks. For each task identify the owner, estimate the time and cost.

This decomposition process will help you develop a schedule for the project plan and the total project cost.

Thank you for purchasing this book and best of luck with your project management adventures.

ABOUT THE AUTHOR

Sadiq Somjee has been in the information technology industry for over thirty years, building, developing and managing technology solutions. He has worked for small companies and large corporations where he has delivered many successful projects. He is an IT management consultant, a software engineer and a graphic novelist.

Project Experience

2014-2016: Project portfolio management including data warehouse, BI, field automation and mobile technology.

2012-2014: Project Manager for a legacy system replacement with a CRM system that included financial, document and call center integrations.

2005-2012: Project portfolio management for a number of enterprise systems including hosting, staffing and outsourcing.

1999-2005: Project manager for a geographically distributed enterprise log inventory system. Help desk practice development and product development software engineering director.

1996-1999: Replacement of an enterprise wide GIS system for a large forestry company.

Roles prior to 1996: Software developer, technical project manager, database administrator and business analyst.

somjeeNotes.blogspot.ca

OTHER BOOKS BY THE AUTHOR

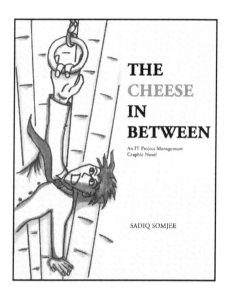

The Cheese in Between is a graphic novel about Max, a newly appointed project manager. He is a simple farm boy who ends up in a big city working for Megacorp. On his journey to complete his assignment, he encounters tribes of managers, developers and consultants. The office ecosystem is indeed a strange place for Max to comprehend, but he must adapt and survive. This is his story.

somjeeNotes.blogspot.ca

50387219R00089

Made in the USA
San Bernardino, CA
27 August 2019